Administration
of Communion
of the Sick

from Pastoral Care of the Sick

Bilingual Edition

United States Co............................ ;
Washington D.C.

ISBN 1-57455-303-8

First Printing, April 1999
Third Printing, April 2002

Communion of the Sick

INTRODUCTION

Whoever eats this bread will live for ever.

71.   This chapter contains two rites: one for use when communion can be celebrated in the context of a liturgy of the word; the other, a brief communion rite for use in more restrictive circumstances, such as in hospitals.

72.   Priests with pastoral responsibilities should see to it that the sick or aged, even though not seriously ill or in danger of death, are given every opportunity to receive the eucharist frequently, even daily, especially during the Easter season. They may receive communion at any hour. Those who care for the sick may receive communion with them, in accord with the usual norms. To provide frequent communion for the sick, it may be necessary to ensure that the community has a sufficient number of ministers of communion.

The communion minister should wear attire appropriate to this ministry.

The sick person and others may help to plan the celebration, for example, by choosing the prayers and readings. Those making these choices should keep in mind the condition of the sick person. The readings and the homily should help those present to reach a deeper understanding of the mystery of human suffering in relation to the paschal mystery of Christ.

73. The faithful who are ill are deprived of their rightful and accustomed place in the eucharistic community. In bringing communion to them the minister of communion represents Christ and manifests faith and charity on behalf of the whole community toward those who cannot be present at the eucharist. For the sick the reception of communion is not only a privilege but also a sign of support and concern shown by the Christian community for its members who are ill.

The links between the community's eucharistic celebration, especially on the Lord's Day, and the communion of the sick are intimate and manifold. Besides remembering the sick in the general intercessions at Mass, those present should be reminded occasionally of the significance of communion in the lives of those who are ill: union with Christ in his struggle with evil, his prayer for the world, and his love for the Father, and union with the community from which they are separated.

The obligation to visit and comfort those who cannot take part in the eucharistic assembly may be clearly demonstrated by taking communion to them from the community's eucharistic celebration. This symbol of unity between the community and its sick members has the deepest significance on the Lord's Day, the special day of the eucharistic assembly.

74.   When the eucharist is brought to the sick, it should be carried in a pyx or small closed container. Those who are with the sick should be asked to prepare a table covered with a linen cloth upon which the blessed sacrament will be placed. Lighted candles are prepared and, where it is customary, a vessel of holy water. Care should be taken to make the occasion special and joyful.

Sick people who are unable to receive under the form of bread may receive under the form of wine alone. If the wine is consecrated at a Mass not celebrated in the presence of the sick person, the blood of the Lord is kept in a properly covered vessel and is placed in the tabernacle after communion. The precious blood should be carried to the sick in a vessel which is closed in such a way as to eliminate all danger of spilling. If some of the precious blood remains, it should be consumed by the minister, who should also see to it that the vessel is properly purified.

75. If the sick wish to celebrate the sacrament of penance, it is preferable that the priest make himself available for this during a previous visit.

76. If it is necessary to celebrate the sacrament of penance during the rite of communion, it takes the place of the penitential rite.

COMMUNION IN ORDINARY CIRCUMSTANCES

77. If possible, provision should be made to celebrate Mass in the homes of the sick, with their families and friends gathered around them. The Ordinary determines the conditions and requirements for such celebrations.

COMMUNION IN A HOSPITAL
OR INSTITUTION

78.   There will be situations, particularly in large institutions with many communicants, when the minister should consider alternative means so that the rite of communion of the sick is not diminished to the absolute minimum. In such cases the following alternatives should be considered: (a) where possible, the residents or patients may be gathered in groups in one or more areas; (b) additional ministers of communion may assist.

When it is not possible to celebrate the full rite, the rite for communion in a hospital or institution may be used. If it is convenient, however, the minister may add elements from the rite for ordinary circumstances, for example, a Scripture reading.

79.   The rite begins with the recitation of the eucharistic antiphon in the church, the hospital chapel, or the first room visited. Then the minister gives communion to the sick in their individual rooms.

80.   The concluding prayer may be said in the church, the hospital chapel, or the last room visited. No blessing is given.

Comunión en Circunstancias Ordinarias

ESQUEMA DEL RITO

RITOS INTRODUCTORIOS
Saludo
Aspersión con agua bendita
Rito penitencial

LITURGIA DE LA PALABRA
Lectura
Respuesta a la Palabra
Preces

LITURGIA DE LA COMUNIÓN
Padrenuestro
Comunión
Oración en silencio
Oración después de la comunión

RITO CONCLUSIVO
Bendición

Communion in Ordinary Circumstances

OUTLINE OF THE RITE

INTRODUCTORY RITES
Greeting
Sprinkling with Holy Water
Penitential Rite

LITURGY OF THE WORD
Reading
Response
General Intercessions

LITURGY OF HOLY COMMUNION
Lord's Prayer
Communion
Silent Prayer
Prayer after Communion

CONCLUDING RITE
Blessing

Comunión en Circunstancias Ordinarias

RITOS INTRODUCTORIOS

SALUDO

81.   El ministro saluda a la persona enferma y a los presentes.

La paz del Señor esté siempre con ustedes.

R.   **Y también contigo.**

Entonces el ministro coloca el Santísimo Sacramento en la mesa y todos juntos lo adoran.

ASPERSIÓN CON AGUA BENDITA

82.   Si parece conveniente, el sacerdote o el diácono rocía con agua bendita a la persona enferma y a todos los presentes.

Communion
in Ordinary
Circumstances

INTRODUCTORY RITES

GREETING

81. The minister greets the sick person and the others present.

The peace of the Lord be with you always.

R. And also with you.

The minister then places the blessed sacrament on the table, and all join in adoration.

SPRINKLING WITH HOLY WATER

82. If it seems desirable, the priest or deacon may sprinkle the sick person and those present with holy water.

Que esta agua bendita nos recuerde el bautismo
que recibimos y renueve nuestra fe en Cristo,
que con su muerte y resurrección nos redimió.

Si tiene lugar aquí el sacramento de la penitencia, se
omite el rito penitencial.

RITO PENITENCIAL

83.   El ministro invita a la persona enferma y a todos
los presentes a participar en el rito penitencial, con estas
u otras palabras parecidas:

Hermanos y hermanas, para
prepararnos a esta celebración,
reconozcamos nuestros pecados.

Después de un breve momento de silencio, prosigue el
rito penitencial.

Señor Jesús, que curaste a los enfermos:
Señor, ten piedad de nosotros.

R.   Señor, ten piedad de nosotros.

Señor Jesús, que perdonaste a los pecadores:
Cristo, ten piedad de nosotros.

R.   Cristo, ten piedad de nosotros.

Let this water call to mind our baptism into Christ, who by his death and resurrection has redeemed us.

If the sacrament of penance is now celebrated, the penitential rite is omitted.

PENITENTIAL RITE

83.   The minister invites the sick person and all present to join in the penitential rite, using these or similar words:

My brothers and sisters, to prepare ourselves for this celebration, let us call to mind our sins.

After a brief period of silence, the penitential rite continues.

Lord Jesus, you healed the sick:
Lord, have mercy.

R.   Lord, have mercy.

Lord Jesus, you forgave sinners:
Christ, have mercy.

R.   Christ, have mercy.

Señor Jesús, que te entregaste a la muerte
para sanarnos y darnos fortaleza: Señor, ten
piedad de nosotros.

R.   Señor ten piedad de nosotros.

El ministro concluye el rito penitencial, diciendo:

El Señor todopoderoso tenga misericordia
de nosotros, perdone nuestros pecados y nos
lleve a la vida eterna.

R.   Amén.

Lord Jesus, you give us yourself to heal us
    and bring us strength:
Lord, have mercy.

R.   Lord, have mercy.

The minister concludes the penitential rite with the
following:

May almighty God have mercy on us,
forgive us our sins,
and bring us to everlasting life.

R.   Amen.

LITURGIA DE LA PALABRA

LECTURA

84.   Uno de los presentes o el ministro proclama la palabra de Dios.

Lectura del santo Evangelio según
   San Juan   6.51

Jesús dice:
"Yo soy el pan vivo que ha bajado del cielo;
el que coma de este pan vivirá para siempre.
Y el pan que yo les voy a dar es mi carne
para que el mundo tenga vida."

Esta es palabra de Dios.

RESPUESTA A LA PALABRA

85.   Se puede guardar un breve espacio de silencio, después de la lectura de la palabra de Dios.

El ministro podrá explicar brevemente la lectura y aplicarla a las necesidades de la persona enferma y de los que cuidan de ella.

LITURGY OF THE WORD

READING

84.   The word of God is proclaimed by one of those present or by the minister.

A reading from the holy gospel
    according to John   6:51

Jesus says:
"I am the living bread that came down from heaven; whoever eats this bread will live forever; and the bread that I will give is my flesh for the life of the world."

This is the Gospel of the Lord.

RESPONSE

85.   A brief period of silence may be observed after the reading of the word of God.

The minister may then give a brief explanation of the reading, applying it to the needs of the sick person and those who are looking after him or her.

PRECES

86.   Se pueden enunciar las peticiones generales.
Mediante una breve introducción, el ministro invita a
todos a orar. Después de las intenciones, el ministro
recita la oración conclusiva. Es recomendable que una
persona distinta del ministro pronuncie las
intenciones.

GENERAL INTERCESSIONS

86. The general intercessions may be said. With a brief introduction the minister invites all those present to pray. After the intentions the minister says the concluding prayer. It is desirable that the intentions be announced by someone other than the minister.

LITURGIA DE LA COMUNIÓN

PADRENUESTRO

87.   El ministro introduce la oración del Señor con estas u otras palabras:

Oremos confiadamente al Padre con las palabras que nos enseñó nuestro Salvador:

Todos dicen:

Padre nuestro . . .

COMUNIÓN

88.   El ministro presenta el pan eucarístico a los presentes, con estas palabras:

Este es el pan de la vida.
Prueben y vean qué bueno es el Señor.

La persona enferma y todos los que vayan a recibir la comunión dicen:

LITURGY OF
HOLY COMMUNION

LORD'S PRAYER

87.   The minister introduces the Lord's Prayer in
these or similar words:

Now let us pray as Christ the Lord has
taught us:

All say:

Our Father . . .

COMMUNION

88.   The minister shows the eucharistic bread to
those present, saying:

This is the bread of life.
Taste and see that the Lord is good.

The sick person and all who are to receive
communion say:

Señor, yo no soy digno de que vengas a mí,
pero una palabra tuya bastará para sanarme.

El ministro se acerca a la persona enferma y
presentándole la sagrada forma, dice:

El Cuerpo de Cristo.

La persona enferma responde "Amén" y recibe la
comunión.

Enseguida el ministro dice:

La Sangre de Cristo.

La persona enferma responde: "Amén" y recibe la
comunión.

Si algunas otras personas presentes quieren comulgar, lo
hacen en la forma acostumbrada.

Terminado el rito, el ministro purifica los vasos
sagrados, como de costumbre.

ORACIÓN EN SILENCIO

89.   Se puede orar aquí en silencio.

Lord, I am not worthy to receive you,
but only say the word and I shall be healed.

The minister goes to the sick person and, showing the blessed sacrament, says:

The body of Christ.

The sick person answers: "**Amen,**" and receives communion.

Then the minister says:

The blood of Christ.

The sick person answers: "**Amen,**" and receives communion.

Others present who wish to receive communion then do so in the usual way.

After the conclusion of the rite, the minister cleanses the vessel as usual.

SILENT PRAYER

89.   Then a period of silence may be observed.

ORACIÓN DESPUÉS DE LA COMUNIÓN

90. El ministro reza la oración conclusiva.

Oremos.

Pausa para orar en silencio, si no se ha hecho anteriormente.

Señor y Padre nuestro,
que nos has llamado a participar
del mismo pan y del mismo vino,
para vivir así unidos a Cristo.
Ayúdanos a vivir unidos a él,
para que produzcamos fruto,
experimentando el gozo de su redención.
Por Cristo, nuestro Señor.

R. Amén.

PRAYER AFTER COMMUNION

90.　The minister says a concluding prayer.

Let us pray.

Pause for silent prayer, if this has not preceded.

God our Father,
you have called us to share the one bread
　　and one cup
and so become one in Christ.

Help us to live in him
that we may bear fruit,
rejoicing that he has redeemed the world.

We ask this through Christ our Lord.

R.　Amen.

RITO CONCLUSIVO

BENDICIÓN

91. El sacerdote o el diácono bendice a la persona enferma y a los presentes. Pero, en el caso de que hayan quedado algunas formas consagradas, puede bendecir al enfermo, haciendo, en silencio, la señal de la cruz con el Santísimo Sacramento.

Que Dios Padre te bendiga.

R.   Amén.

Que Dios Hijo te cure.

R.   Amén.

Que Dios Espíritu Santo te ilumine.

R.   Amén.

Que te bendiga Dios todopoderoso,
Padre, Hijo + y Espíritu Santo.

R. Amén.

CONCLUDING RITE

BLESSING

91. The priest or deacon blesses the sick person and the others present. If, however, any of the blessed sacrament remains, he may bless the sick person by making a sign of the cross with the blessed sacrament, in silence.

May God the Father bless you.

R. Amen.

May God the Son heal you.

R. Amen.

May God the Holy Spirit enlighten you.

R. Amen.

May almighty God bless you, the Father, and the Son, + and the Holy Spirit.

R. Amen.

Si el ministro no es sacerdote ni diácono, invoca la bendición de Dios y hace sobre sí mismo(a) la señal de la cruz, diciendo:

Que el Señor nos bendiga,
nos libre de todo mal
y nos lleve a la vida eterna.

R.   Amén.

A minister who is not a priest or deacon invokes God's blessing and makes the sign of the cross on himself or herself, while saying:

May the Lord bless us,
protect us from all evil,
and bring us to everlasting life.

R.   Amen.

Comunión en un Hospital u Otra Institución

ESQUEMA DEL RITO

RITO INTRODUCTORIO
Antífona

LITURGIA DE LA COMUNIÓN
Saludo
Padrenuestro
Comunión

RITO CONCLUSIVO
Oración final

Communion in a Hospital or Institution

OUTLINE OF THE RITE

INTRODUCTORY RITE
Antiphon

LITURGY OF HOLY COMMUNION
Greeting
Lord's Prayer
Communion

CONCLUDING RITE
Concluding Prayer

Comunión en un Hospital u Otra Institución

RITO INTRODUCTORIO

ANTÍFONA

92. El rito puede iniciarse en el templo, en la capilla del hospital o en el primer cuarto, en donde el sacerdote recita la siguiente antífona:

¡Oh sagrado banquete
donde Cristo es alimento!
Se recuerda su pasión,
el alma se llena de gracia,
se nos da en prenda
la gloria futura.

Si se acostumbra, el ministro puede ir acompañado por una persona que lleve una vela.

Communion in a Hospital or Institution

INTRODUCTORY RITE

ANTIPHON

92.   The rite may begin in the church, the hospital chapel, or the first room, where the minister says the following antiphon:

How holy this feast
in which Christ is our food:
his passion is recalled;
grace fills our hearts;
and we receive a pledge of the glory to come.

If it is customary, the minister may be accompanied by a person carrying a candle.

LITURGIA DE LA COMUNIÓN

SALUDO

93.   Al entrar en cada habitación, el ministro puede recitar el siguiente saludo:

Que la paz del Señor esté siempre con ustedes.

R.   Y también contigo.

El ministro coloca el Santísimo Sacramento en la mesa y todos juntos lo adoran.

Sí hay tiempo y parece conveniente, el ministro puede proclamar la Palabra.

PADRENUESTRO

94.   Si las circunstancias lo permiten (por ejemplo, si no son muchas las salas que hay que visitar), es muy conveniente que el ministro guíe a los enfermos en la recitación del Padrenuestro. Puede hacerlo con éstas o semejantes palabras:

LITURGY OF HOLY COMMUNION

GREETING

93. On entering each room, the minister may use the following greeting:

The peace of the Lord be with you always.

R. And also with you.

The minister then places the blessed sacrament on the table, and all join in adoration.

If there is time and it seems desirable, the minister may proclaim a Scripture reading.

LORD'S PRAYER

94. When circumstances permit (for example, when there are not many rooms to visit), the minister is encouraged to lead the sick in the Lord's Prayer. The minister introduces the Lord's Prayer in these or similar words:

Jesús nos enseñó a llamar Padre a Dios;
por eso nos atrevemos a decir:

Todos dicen:

Padre nuestro . . .

COMUNIÓN

95.   El ministro muestra el pan eucarístico a los
presentes, diciendo:

Este es el Cordero de Dios
que quita el pecado del mundo.
¡Dichosos los que tienen hambre y sed,
porque ellos están saciados!

La persona enferma y todos aquellos que vayan a
comulgar dicen:

Señor, yo no soy digno de que vengas a mí,
pero una palabra tuya bastará para sanarme.

El ministro se acerca a la persona enferma, le muestra
la hostia, diciéndole:

El Cuerpo de Cristo.

Jesus taught us to call God our Father, and so we have the courage to say:

All say:

Our Father . . .

COMMUNION

95. The minister shows the eucharistic bread to those present, saying:

This is the Lamb of God
who takes away the sins of the world.
Happy are those who hunger and thirst,
for they shall be satisfied.

The sick person and all who are to receive communion say:

Lord, I am not worthy to receive you,
but only say the word and I shall be healed.

The minister goes to the sick person and, showing the blessed sacrament, says:

The body of Christ.

La persona enferma responde: "**Amén**", y recibe la comunión.

Entonces el ministro dice:

La Sangre de Cristo.

La persona enferma responde: "**Amén**", y recibe la comunión.

Las demás personas que quieran comulgar reciben la comunión en la forma acostumbrada.

The sick person answers: "Amen," and receives communion.

Then the minister says:

The blood of Christ.

The sick person answers: "Amen," and receives communion.

Others present who wish to receive communion then do so in the usual way.

RITO CONCLUSIVO

ORACIÓN CONCLUSIVA

96. La oración conclusiva puede recitarse en el último salón o habitación o en la iglesia o en la capilla.

Oremos.

Pausa para orar en silencio.

Señor y Padre nuestro,
que nos has llamado a participar
del mismo pan y del mismo vino,
para vivir así unidos a Cristo,
ayúdanos a vivir unidos a él,
para que produzcamos fruto,
experimentando el gozo de su redención.
Por Cristo, nuestro Señor.

R. Amén.

Se omite la bendición y el ministro purifica los vasos sagrados como de costumbre.

CONCLUDING RITE

CONCLUDING PRAYER

96.   The concluding prayer may be said either in the last room visited, in the church, or chapel.

Let us pray.

Pause for silent prayer.

God our Father,
you have called us to share the one bread
      and one cup
and so become one in Christ.

Help us to live in him
that we may bear fruit,
rejoicing that he has redeemed the world.

We ask this through Christ our Lord.

R.   Amen.

The blessing is omitted and the minister cleanses the vessel as usual.